BUILDING A HIGHWAY

BY KAREN LATCHANA KENNEY

SEQUENCE

AMICUS | AMICUS INK

Sequence is published by Amicus and Amicus Ink
P.O. Box 1329, Mankato, MN 56002
www.amicuspublishing.us

Library of Congress Cataloging-in-Publication Data
Names: Kenney, Karen Latchana, author.
Title: Building a highway / by Karen Latchana Kenney.
Description: Mankato, MN : Amicus and Amicus Ink, [2020] | Series: Sequence amazing structures | Includes index. | Audience: Grades 4 to 6
Identifiers: LCCN 2019006196 (print) | LCCN 2019007837 (ebook) | ISBN 9781681518749 (pdf) | ISBN 9781681518343 (library binding) | ISBN 9781681525624 (pbk.)
Subjects: LCSH: Highway engineering--Juvenile literature.
Classification: LCC TE149 (ebook) | LCC TE149 .K46 2020 (print) | DDC 625.7--dc23
LC record available at https://lccn.loc.gov/2019006196

Editor: Wendy Dieker
Designer: Ciara Beitlich
Photo Researcher: Shane Freed

Photo Credits: Getty/PhotoAlto/Jerome Gorin cover; Getty/Hisham Ibrahim 5; iStock/sefa ozel 6; iStock/flyfloor 6; iStock/BartCo 9; Shutterstock/watchara panyajun 10–11; Getty/seksan/Mongkhonkhamsao 13; iStock/tolgart 14–15; iStock/ewg3D 16; iStock/Altitude Drone 18–19; Shutterstock/Kritthaneth 20; iStock/getty_dumy67 22–23; iStock/i-Stockr 24–25; iStock/Andyqwe 26–27; Getty/Pavliha 29

Printed in the United States of America

HC 10 9 8 7 6 5 4 3 2 1
PB 10 9 8 7 6 5 4 3 2 1

TABLE OF CONTENTS

We Need a Highway

It's summer! It's time to take a road trip and see places far from home. The roads go through many towns. These routes are clogged with cars. Wouldn't it be nice to go around the town? Yes! A road around the town would make the trip faster. We can drive faster on an open road. We need a highway.

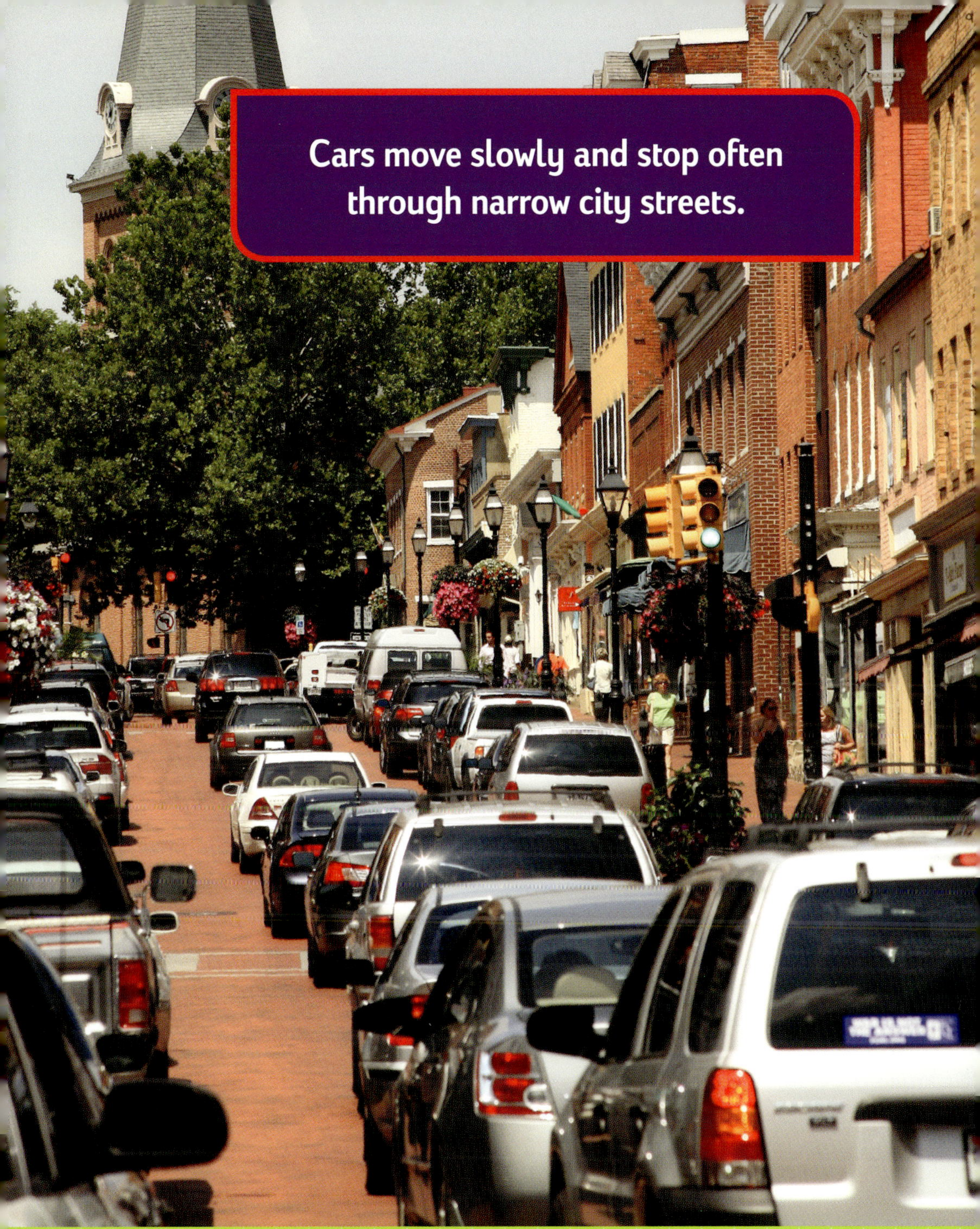

Cars move slowly and stop often through narrow city streets.

...LOADING... LOADING... LOADING...

Road planners look at charts and information about traffic patterns.

The state makes a plan to build a highway.

YEAR 1

LOADING . . . LOADING . .

Road Planning

Highways take many years to build. The first step is to make a plan. A state's Department of Transportation (DOT) looks at traffic and crash **data**. Their plan says the new highway will be faster and safer for drivers in the area.

The DOT also looks at the **budget**. This says how much **tax money** the DOT can use to build the highway.

OADING . . . LOADING . . . LOADING . . .

The state government likes the plan. They hire **engineers** to get to work. Engineers look at the soil. They see what is in the way of the planned highway. They also look at the **environment**. Will plants and animals be harmed by a highway? Will traffic be too noisy for people living there?

Engineers take soil samples from the land where the new highway might go.

The state makes a plan to build a highway.

YEAR 1

YEAR 2

ING . . . LOADING . . .

Engineers study the land and areas where the highway will go.

OADING . . . LOADING . . . LOADING . . .

Engineers draw maps and designs of the new highway.

The state makes a plan to build a highway.

YEAR 1

Engineers study the land and areas where the highway will go.

YEAR 2

Engineers design the highway. The state buys land.

YEAR 4

. . LOADING . .

After the land study, engineers make a design of the highway. They look at the budget. The engineers decide if the highway should have two or four lanes. They decide where turn lanes should go. They present a map and designs to the state. The state likes the design. It starts buying the land it needs for the highway.

Preparing for the Build

Now the state needs to find a **contractor**. A contractor is a company that will build the highway. Contractors have big construction machines. They hire the workers.

Different contractors make **proposals**. A proposal tells the contractor's plan. It says how long the project will take and how much it will cost. The state picks one of the contractors to do the work.

YEAR 1: The state makes a plan to build a highway.

YEAR 2: Engineers study the land and areas where the highway will go.

YEAR 4: Engineers design the highway. The state buys land.

YEAR 6: The state picks a contractor to build the highway.

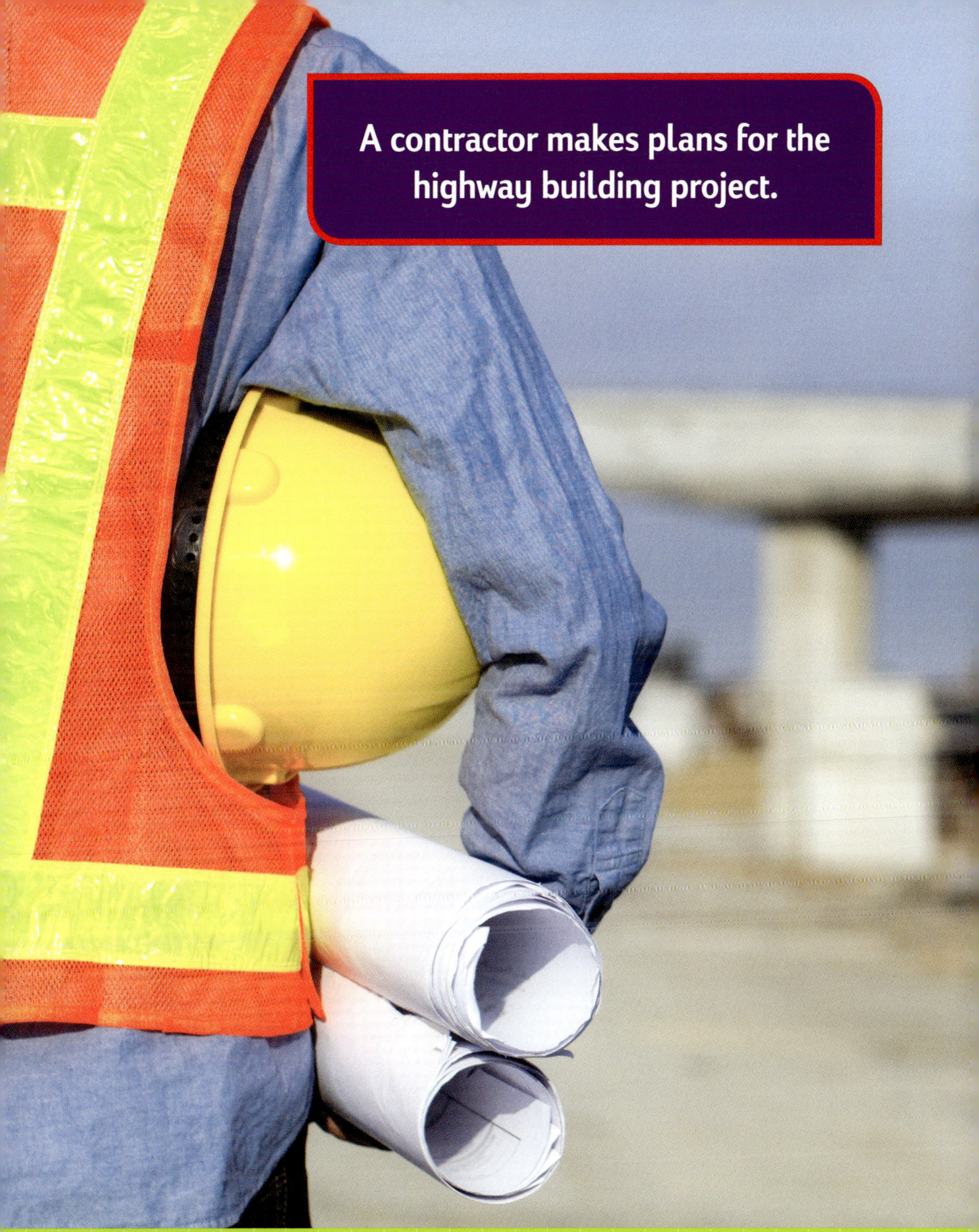

A contractor makes plans for the highway building project.

OADING . . . LOADING . . . LOADING . . .

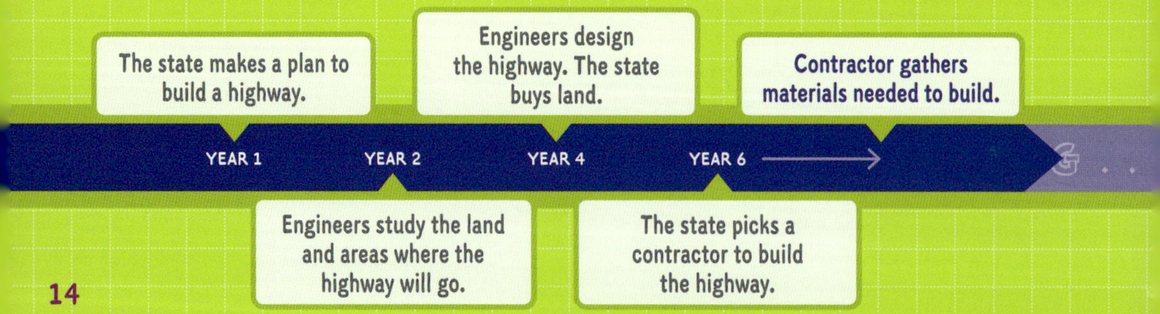
The state makes a plan to build a highway.
Engineers design the highway. The state buys land.
Contractor gathers materials needed to build.
YEAR 1
YEAR 2
YEAR 4
YEAR 6
Engineers study the land and areas where the highway will go.
The state picks a contractor to build the highway.

Highways can be made of **asphalt** or **concrete**. Different materials work better in different places. The engineers decided asphalt would be best for this highway. Asphalt is cheaper and will be ready for drivers sooner. The contractor finds an asphalt supplier. They also get tons of gravel for making base layers of the roadway.

Huge piles of gravel are ready for the highway building project.

An excavator digs up dirt to prepare the roadway.

- **YEAR 1**: The state makes a plan to build a highway.
- **YEAR 2**: Engineers study the land and areas where the highway will go.
- **YEAR 4**: Engineers design the highway. The state buys land.
- **YEAR 6**: The state picks a contractor to build the highway.
- Contractor gathers materials needed to build.
- **YEAR 7**: Workers make the highway's foundation.

Building the Highway

It's been six years of planning. Finally, the contractor can start building! The **foundation** of the road has to be solid and smooth. The road needs ditches along the sides to help drain water away. The workers will do **earthwork** to prepare the land. They use big machines to dig and move dirt. A raised road is starting to take shape.

OADING . . . LOADING . . . LOADING . . .

Next, the workers smooth out the surface of the road. A bulldozer flattens out bumps and fills in holes. But the dirt is filled with small air pockets. To fix this, workers spray the dirt with water. Then they drive a machine with a big roller over the dirt. The roller packs down the wet dirt.

- YEAR 1: The state makes a plan to build a highway.
- YEAR 2: Engineers study the land and areas where the highway will go.
- YEAR 4: Engineers design the highway. The state buys land.
- YEAR 6: The state picks a contractor to build the highway.
- Contractor gathers materials needed to build.
- YEAR 7: Workers make the highway's foundation.

A bulldozer and a roller work to flatten the ground.

Workers level and pack down the dirt.

LOADING... LOADING...

The state makes a plan to build a highway.

YEAR 1

Engineers study the land and areas where the highway will go.

YEAR 2

Engineers design the highway. The state buys land.

YEAR 4

The state picks a contractor to build the highway.

YEAR 6

Contractor gathers materials needed to build.

YEAR 7

Workers make the highway's foundation.

Then workers start shaping the road. It has to be slightly higher in the middle. Then rain will run off and into the ditches along the sides. That's where the builders put storm drains. They bury large pipes along the road. Grates above the ground will let water into the pipes. Then the water flows to areas away from the road.

A system of concrete pipes will catch rain water and drain it away from the new road.

Workers level and pack down the dirt.

DING . . . LOADING . . .

Road is shaped and storm drains are added.

The foundation is ready for its next layer. Workers spread gravel over the soil. Gravel is made of sand and small pieces of rock. Workers wet the gravel and press it down with a roller. They add more layers of gravel. The gravel helps keep water away from the top layer of the highway. This helps the highway last a long time.

Layers of gravel are packed down on top of dirt to prepare for the asphalt.

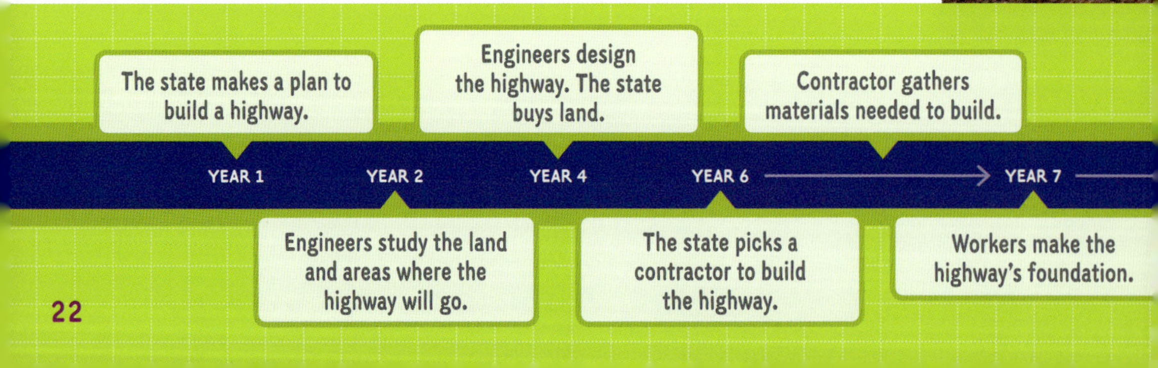

Workers level and pack down the dirt.

Workers layer gravel over the foundation.

YEAR 8

...LOADING...

Road is shaped and storm drains are added.

Now the highway gets its final layer. A paving truck moves over the gravel. It pours a thin layer of asphalt as it moves. The asphalt is hot and soft. It starts to cool down and harden. As it cools, workers drive over it with road rollers. The rollers press down on the asphalt. This makes the road very strong and smooth.

- YEAR 1: The state makes a plan to build a highway.
- YEAR 2: Engineers study the land and areas where the highway will go.
- YEAR 4: Engineers design the highway. The state buys land.
- YEAR 6: The state picks a contractor to build the highway.
- YEAR 6 → YEAR 7: Contractor gathers materials needed to build.
- YEAR 7: Workers make the highway's foundation.

Rollers flatten the hot asphalt into a strong and smooth surface.

Workers level and pack down the dirt.

Road is shaped and storm drains are added.

Workers layer gravel over the foundation.

YEAR 8

Asphalt is laid on top of gravel layers.

OADING . . .

YEAR 1 — The state makes a plan to build a highway.

YEAR 2 — Engineers study the land and areas where the highway will go.

YEAR 4 — Engineers design the highway. The state buys land.

YEAR 6 — The state picks a contractor to build the highway.

Contractor gathers materials needed to build.

YEAR 7 — Workers make the highway's foundation.

The highway is almost finished. But first the DOT tests the new road. The testers drive on the road. Inspectors check the asphalt. Workers fix any problems. Then final touches are added. Workers paint traffic lines on the road. They also plant trees and grass along the sides of the highway.

A line painting truck sprays a fresh coat of yellow and white lines.

Workers level and pack down the dirt.

Road is shaped and storm drains are added.

YEAR 8

Workers layer gravel over the foundation.

Asphalt is laid on top of gravel layers.

YEAR 9

Highway is inspected; lines are painted; trees and grass are planted.

NG . . .

Get on the Highway!

This highway is ready for drivers! It took nine years to plan and build. But now it connects cities and towns. With cars and trucks, people can get around quickly. This highway is ready to take them places. Where do you think they will go?

- YEAR 1: The state makes a plan to build a highway.
- YEAR 2: Engineers study the land and areas where the highway will go.
- YEAR 4: Engineers design the highway. The state buys land.
- YEAR 6: The state picks a contractor to build the highway.
- Contractor gathers materials needed to build.
- YEAR 7: Workers make the highway's foundation.

A new highway makes travel easier and faster for drivers.

Workers level and pack down the dirt.

Road is shaped and storm drains are added.

Workers layer gravel over the foundation.

YEAR 8

Asphalt is laid on top of gravel layers.

Highway is inspected; lines are painted; trees and grass are planted.

YEAR 9

The new highway opens.

GLOSSARY

asphalt A black, tarlike material that is mixed with sand and gravel; it can be used to make the top layer of a highway.

budget A plan for how much money is available and what it will be spent on.

concrete A building material made from sand, gravel, cement, and water.

contractor A company that agrees to build a highway or other construction project; they hire the workers, bring the machines, and finish the project.

data Information or facts gathered.

earthwork Digging and moving soil in order to prepare for a building project, such as a highway.

engineers People trained to plan and design highways and other construction projects.

environment The natural areas of the world.

foundation A solid area on which a highway or other structure is built.

tax money Money the state takes in from the people who live there; people pay taxes to the state so the state can offer services, like building roads and running utility systems.

READ MORE

Furgang, Kathy. *Zoom in on Superhighways.* New York: Enslow Publishing, 2018.

Stefoff, Rebecca. *Building Roads.* New York: Cavendish Square, 2016.

Taylor, Charlotte. *Highways and Roads.* New York: Enslow Publishing, 2019.

WEBSITES

Federal Highway Administration, The Interstate Kids' Section
https://www.fhwa.dot.gov/interstate/brainiacs/

New York State, Traffic Safety Kids Page
http://safeny.ny.gov/kids.htm

Wonderopolis, How Do You Build a Road?
https://wonderopolis.org/wonder/how-do-you-build-a-road

INDEX

ABOUT THE AUTHOR

Author and editor Karen Latchana Kenney has written many science books for children and young adults. She loves taking road trips on the highway to parks and small towns. Karen lives in Minneapolis, Minnesota, with her husband and young son.